The month of March, from the illuminated manuscript
Les Très Riches Heures du duc de Berry

The Story of a Special Day
Volume 84

March

24

83rd day of the year
(84th in leap years)
282 days remaining
until the end of the year.

by Michael Dobson

Timespinner
Press

For more information about the series, about me, or about your special day, please email us at editor@timespinnerpress.com.

Look for other volumes in *The Story of a Special Day*, coming often.

Table of Contents

Cover: Tokugawa Ieyasu, founder of the Tokugawa shogunate that ruled Japan from 1600 to 1868, was made shogun on March 24, 1603, the Event of the Day.

Back Cover and Title Page: The month of March, from the French Gothic illuminated manuscript *Les Très Riches Heures du duc de Berry.*

March 24 Quotations

"Though I be a woman yet I have as good a courage answerable to my place as ever my father had. I am your anointed Queen. I will never be by violence constrained to do anything. I thank God I am endued with such qualities that if I were turned out of the Realm in my petticoat I were able to live in any place in Christendom."

— *Queen Elizabeth I of England, died March 24, 1603*

"I knew, as everyone knows, that the easiest way to attract a crowd is to let it be known that at a given time and a given place some one is going to attempt something that in the event of failure will mean sudden death."

— *escapologist Harry Houdini, born March 24, 1874*

"If we could read the secret history of our enemies, we should find in each man's life sorrow and suffering enough to disarm all hostility."

— *poet Henry Wadsworth Longfellow, died March 24, 1882*

"I don't believe there is any finer mission on earth than just to make people laugh."

— *actor and director Fatty Arbuckle, born March 24, 1887*

"The fact that political ideologies are tangible realities is not a proof of their vitally necessary character. The bubonic plague was an extraordinarily powerful social reality, but no one would have regarded it as vitally necessary."

— *psychologist Wilhelm Reich, born March 24, 1897*

"Now when an American has an idea, he directly seeks a second American to share it. If there be three, they elect a president and two secretaries. Given four, they name a keeper of records, and the office is ready for work; five, they convene a general meeting, and the club is fully constituted."

— *science fiction writer Jules Verne, died March 24, 1905*

"If you take care of your character, your reputation will take care of itself."

— *businessman Alan Sugar, born March 24, 1947*

"There's no chance that the iPhone is going to get any significant market share. No chance."

— *Microsoft CEO Steve Ballmer, born March 24, 1956*

"The US has broken the second rule of war. That is, don't go fighting with your land army on the mainland of Asia. Rule One is don't march on Moscow. I developed these two rules myself."

— *Field Marshal Bernard Montgomery, died March 24, 1976*

Event of the Day

Tokugawa Becomes Shogun of Japan

A reënactor plays Tokugawa in the annual Ieyasu Parade

To American audiences, Tokugawa Ieyasu (January 31, 1543 — June 1, 1616) may be best known as "Toranaga," the Japanese feudal warlord in James Clavell's best-selling 1975 novel *Shōgun*, and the 1980 TV miniseries of the same name, in which he was played by noted Japanese actor Toshiro Mifune.

Shōgun is a fictionalized account of Tokugawa's

rise to power, and although some parts are fanciful, much of the overall story parallels history — including the marooned English navigator "John Blackthorne" (real name: William Adams) played by Richard Chamberlain in the TV series.

A decade-long civil war beginning in 1467 CE tore apart existing Japanese institutions and triggered the century-long "Warring States Period," in which individual feudal lords, known as *daimyo*, engaged in nearly non-stop political intrigue and military conflict that left large swaths of Japan in ruin.

It wasn't until 1573 that some semblance of central government was reestablished under Oda Nobunaga and his successor Toyotomi Hideyoshi. Hideyoshi squandered much of his power attempting to conquer Korea and China, and died of the plague when his son and heir, was only five years old.

Tokugawa was a brilliant military leader and a powerful daimyo. He fought for Nobunaga and Hideyoshi in helping them restore central government, and established his own fortress in the town of Edo (later renamed Tokyo). On Hideyoshi's death, he became a member of the Council of Five Elders, who were supposed to rule until Hideyoshi's son grew to manhood.

With five powerful daimyo, the political situation in Japan once again became unstable. One of the daimyo tried to have Tokugawa killed, but failed.

Both the Mitsunari and the Tokugawa factions met in the most important battle in Japanese history, the Battle of Sekigahara, which took place on October 21, 1600, and involved over 80,000 soldiers on each side. It was a complete and utter victory for Tokugawa. His opponents were crushed (and many killed), and from that time onward, Tokugawa was the supreme power in Japan.

The formal title of *shōgun*, roughly equivalent to generalissimo, was bestowed on Tokugawa by the Japanese Emperor Go-Yōzei on March 24, 1603. The Tokugawa shogunate would rule Japan for over 200 years and give the country the longest period of peace and stability in its history.

During the shogunate, Japan experienced substantial economic growth and a renaissance in art and popular culture. Japan was isolationist, forbidding foreigners except in the single trading city of Nagasaki. While this gave Japanese society stability, it also meant that Japan did not receive the benefits of the rapid industrialization taking place in western Europe.

Troubles slowly mounted for the Tokugawa shogunate, including natural disasters and rebellions. When US Navy Commodore Matthew C. Perry steamed into Edo Bay in July 1853, the shogunate was forced to open Japan to trade with foreigners. This led to the Meiji Restoration in 1868, in which government authority was returned to the Emperor and a council of advisors. Japan embraced industrialization and once again became a regional military power.

March 24 Holidays and Celebrations

Día de la Memoria por la Verdad y la Justici (Argentina)

On March 24, Argentinians celebrate the Day of Remembrance for Truth and Justice as a public holiday, commemorating the victims of the "Dirty War" of the 1970s, in which approximately 22,000 were killed or "disappeared" by the Argentine military. The date of March 24 was chosen because the coup d'état that brought the military government to power took place on March 24, 1976.

World Tuberculosis Day (International)

The World Health Organization and the International Union Against Tuberculosis and Lung Disease sponsor World Tuberculosis Day on March 24 to build public awareness about a global epidemic of the disease that kills nearly 2 million people each year. The date was chosen to commemorate the announcement by Dr. Robert Koch that he had discovered the TB bacillus that causes tuberculosis, which took place on March 24, 1882.

Easter Season

Easter is a "moveable feast," meaning it occurs on different days each year. The earliest date for Easter is March 22. See the Easter Events section for more details.

Christian Feast Days

In Western Christianity, March 24 is the feast day of Catherine of Vadstena and Mac Cairthinn of Clogher.

In Eastern Orthodox Christianity, it's also the commemoration of Saint Zacharias the Recluse, Saint Ancmon, Saint James the Confessor, Hieromartyr Parthcnius, martyrs Stephen and Peter of Kazan, Saint Artemius, Saint Zachariah, Saint Savvas the New of Kalymnos, Saint Martin of Thebes, and the Martyrs of Caesarea.

(These Eastern Orthodox events are observed on April 5 by "Old Calendarists" who use the Julian calendar.)

What Happened on March 24?

The abbreviation "O.S." on some dates refers to the fact that the Russian Empire did not switch from the Julian to the Gregorian calendar at the same time as the rest of Europe, and therefore some figures and events have two dates.

People and events whose original names are not in the Western alphabet have their native names (where possible) in the appropriate script shown in parenthesis. These characters may not display on all devices.

1601 CE – Union of England and Scotland

King James VI of Scotland was only 18 months old when his mother, Mary Queen of Scots was forced to abdicate the throne. Because Mary Queen of Scots was the sister of the childless Queen Elizabeth I of England and Ireland, James IV became King of Great Britain on March 24, 1603, following the death of Elizabeth.

Because England had never had a King James, the new monarch was styled James VI and I, King of Great Britain and Ireland. His reign was known as the Jacobean era. James VI and I sponsored the translation of the Bible known as the Authorized King James Version.

While the crowns of of the two countries were united under James VI and I, full political union of Great Britain and Scotland would not take place for nearly a century.

James VI and I by Daniel Mytens

1765 CE – **Quartering Act Becomes Law**

On March 24, 1765, the English Parliament passed and the King signed the Quartering Act of 1765, which required the American colonists to provide housing for British soldiers. Colonial resistance to the Act was so great that it was allowed to expire two years later.

The Quartering Act is seen as one of the "Intolerable Acts" that led the colonists to rebel against England and form their own country, and is listed as one of the grievances in the Declaration of Independence. The Third Amendment to the US Constitution forbidding the quartering of troops in private homes without consent has its origins in the Quartering Act.

1832 CE –**Joseph Smith is Tarred and Feathered**

Joseph Smith, Jr., was founder of the Latter Day Saint movement, more commonly known as Mormonism. He and his followers settled in Ohio and Missouri in the 1830s, but conflicts within the church and with the community led to trouble.

On the night of March 24, 1832, a mob broke down his front door and dragged him from his bedroom. Smith was strangled, beaten, poisoned, and tarred and feathered by his attackers, who left him for dead.

He was able to make it back to a supporter's house and eventually recovered from his wounds. His infant child was knocked onto the floor and left in the cold, and died of exposure five days later.

1837 CE –**Black Canadians Get Voting Rights**

Canada, the destination for many slaves who escaped via the Underground Railway, extended the voting franchise to black men on March 24, 1837. Women (of any color) received voting rights in 1918.

1922 CE –**McMahon Murders in Northern Ireland**

On March 24, 1922, Ulster police officers broke into the home of the McMahon family and shot eight men, killing all but two. The murders were apparently reprisals for an Irish Republican Army (IRA) killing of two policemen the previous day. None of the eight men were involved in the IRA killing, or even involved with the IRA or its political arm Sinn Féin. While suspicion has fallen on specific police officers, no one was ever charged or convicted.

1934 CE – **The Philippines Become Self-Governing**

The Philippine Independence Act, also known as the Tydings-McDuffie Act, was passed by Congress and signed into law by the President on March 24, 1934.

It provided for self-government of the Philippines under its own constitution, and for full independence within ten years.

1944 CE – **The Great Escape**

On the night of March 24-25, 1944, after nearly a year of planning and hard work, Allied airmen began a daring escape from the German POW camp Stalag Luft III, made famous by the 1963 movie *The Great Escape*. Over 200 POWs were selected to join the escape, but only 76 made it out before the guards caught on. Of them, 73 were recaptured, and 50 of those were murdered by the Gestapo at the direct order of Adolf Hitler.

1958 CE – **Elvis is Drafted**

On March 24, 1958, Elvis Presley was inducted into the United States Army as private. Although he was mobbed as he stepped from the bus, he told the crowd that he was looking forward to his service and did not wish to be treated differently from other soldiers. He donated his Army pay to charity, purchased TV sets for his base in Germany, and bought an extra set of fatigues for every one in his unit. Elvis had recorded a number of songs prior to being drafted, and so had ten Top 40 hits during his enlistment. He was honorably discharged on March 5, 1960.

Elvis Presley in *Jailhouse Rock*

1965 CE – **Launch of Ranger 9**

Ranger 9, designed to crash onto the lunar surface while transmitting high-resolution photographs, crashed into the Moon on March 24, 1965, 64.5 hours after its launch, sending back a number of high quality images of the lunar surface.

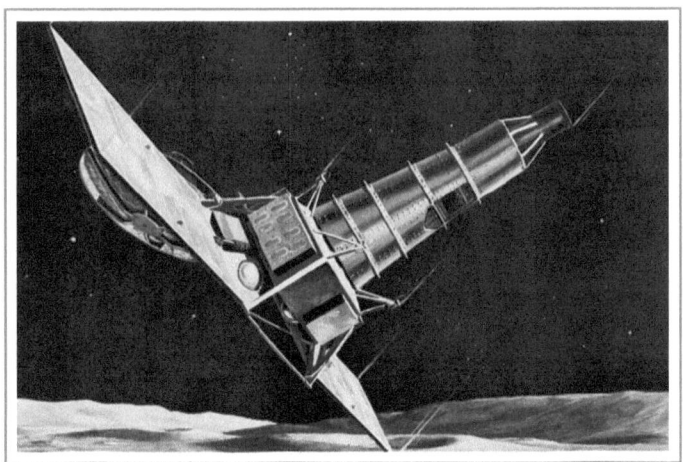

Ranger 9 about to impact on the Moon

1989 CE – *Exxon Valdez* Oil Spill

On March 24, 1989, the *Exxon Valdez*, carrying about 55 million gallons of oil from the Prudhoe Bay oil field, struck Bligh Reef in Prince William Sound, Alaska. The resultant spill released at least 11 million gallons of oil, which spread to cover 11,000 square miles of ocean and 1,300 miles of coastline, killing hundreds of thousands of animals.

1993 CE – Comet Shoemaker-Levy 9 Discovered

At the Palomar Observatory on the night of March 24, 1993, astronomers Carolyn and Eugene Shoemaker and David Levy discovered a comet that had been captured by Jupiter's gravitational field.

Shoemaker-Levy 9 broke apart and collided with the planet Jupiter the following year in the first directly observed extraterrestrial collision of Solar System objects.

Comet Shoemaker-Levy 9 colliding with Jupiter,
painted by Don Davis

Who Was Born on March 24?

Art, Cartooning, and Design

Tommy Hilfiger (March 24, 1951 —)

Fashion designer Tommy Hilfiger built the lifestyle brand that bears his name.

Bob Mackie (March 24, 1940 —)

Fashion designer Bob Mackie is known for costuming Cher, Judy Garland, Liza Minnelli, Tina Turner, and many other popular icons. He designed costumes for The Carol Burnett Show, the 1993 television adaptation of Gypsy, and many others. He won nine Emmy Awards and received three Academy Award nomination for his work.

Joseph Barbera (March 24, 1911 — December 18, 2006)

Animator Joseph Barbera co-founded Hanna-Barbera studios, which produced *The Flintstones, Scooby-Doo, Yogi Bear, The Smurfs*, and *The Jetsons*. William Hanna and Joseph Barbera together won seven Oscars and eight Emmys.

Ub Iwerks (March 24, 1901 — July 7, 1971)

Ub Iwerks co-created Mickey Mouse and Oswald the Lucky Rabbit with his partner Walt Disney. He invented several special visual effects techniques, designed theme park attractions, and won an Academy Award for developing the special effects for Alfred Hitchcock's 1963 film *The Birds*.

Edward Weston (March 24, 1886 — January 1, 1958)

American photographer Edward Weston is known as "one of the masters of 20th century photography." He was the first photographer to receive a Guggenheim Fellowship.

Edward Weston and Marguerite Mather, photograph by Imogen Cunningham

Orest Kiprensky (Орест Кипренский) (March 24 [O.S. March 13], 1782 — October 17 [O.S. October 5], 1836)

Kiprensky was a Russian painter of portraits during the Age of Romanticism.

Orest Kiprensky, self portrait, 1828

Business

Steve Ballmer (March 24, 1956 —)

Ballmer became CEO of Microsoft Corporation in 2000.

Steve Ballmer

Alan Sugar (March 24, 1947 —)

British businessman Sugar built a fortune of £770m (US$1.14 billion) for his involvement in such companies as Amstrad and Tottenham Hotspur. He hosted the BBC version of the TV series *The Apprentice*. He was knighted in 2000 and made a baron in 2009.

Andrew W. Mellon (March 24 1855 — August 26, 1937)

Banker and industrialist Mellon was the third highest income tax payer in the US, behind John D. Rockefeller and Henry Ford. He was later Secretary of the Treasury for eleven years, surviving an impeachment attempt after the onset of the Great Depression. A noted art collector, his collection (and a $10 million construction fund, the equivalent of $160 million today) form the basis of the National Gallery of Art.

George Francis Train (March 24 1829 — January 5, 1904)

American businessman George Train (right) built the Union Pacific Railroad and the Credit Mobilier, along with a clipper ship line and a horse tramway company. He ran for President of the United States in 1872 as an independent, and was jailed for defending Victoria Woodhull's decision for reporting on the affair of Henry Ward Beecher and Elizabeth Tilton.

Crime and Punishment

Clyde Barrow (March 24, 1909 — May 23, 1934)

Outlaw Clyde Barrow led the "Barrow Gang," which committed over a dozen bank robberies and killed nine police officers. With his girlfriend Bonnie Parker, the two were immortalized in Arthur Penn's 1967 film *Bonnie and Clyde*. They were ambushed and killed in Louisiana by police in 1934.

Clyde Barrow and Bonnie Parker

Film, Television, and Theater

Lake Bell (March 24, 1979 —)

Bell had starring roles in the TV series *The Practice* and *Boston Legal*, and appeared in numerous films.

Jessica Chastain (March 24, 1977 —)

Chastain was nominated for an Oscar and a Golden Globe for *The Help*, and won a Golden globe and an Oscar nomination for *Zero Dark Thirty*. She was named one of the "100 Most Influential People in the World" by *Time* magazine in 2012.

Alyson Hannigan (March 24, 1974 —)

Hannigan is known for playing Willow in *Buffy the Vampire Slayer*, Lily on *How I Met Your Mother*, and Michelle in the *American Pie* films.

Alyson Hannigan (right) with Amber Benson.
Photo: Raven Underwood

Jim Parsons (March 24, 1973 —)

Parsons is best known for his role as Sheldon Cooper on the sitcom *The Big Bang Theory.*

Megyn Price (March 24, 1971 —)

Price appeared on the sitcoms *Grounded for Life* and *Rules of Engagement.*

Lara Flynn Boyle (March 24, 1970 —)

Boyle is known for her roles in *Twin Peaks* and *The Practice*, and appeared as the villain in the film *Men In Black II.*

Peter Jacobson (March 24, 1965 —)

Jacobson is best known as a regular on the TV series *House.*

Star Jones (March 24, 1962 —)

Lawyer and television personality Star Jones is best known as a co-host of the talk show *The View.*

Kelly LeBrock (March 24, 1960 —)

Supermodel Kelly LeBrock is best known for her roles *in The Woman in Red* and *Weird Science.*

Donna Pescow (March 24, 1954 —)

Pescow is best known for her role in the John Travolta film *Saturday Night Fever*. She played Dr. Lynn Carlson on *All My Children*, the first lesbian character on a daytime soap opera, and appeared in other soap operas including *One Life to Live* and *General Hospital.*

Robert Carradine (March 24, 1954 —)

A member of the Carradine family of actors, Robert Carradine is best known for his role in the *Revenge of the Nerds* film series and as the father on the Disney Channel sitcom *Lizzie McGuire.*

Louie Anderson (March 24, 1953 —)

Comedian Louie Anderson is known for his stand-up work, for his cartoon series *Life With Louie*, and as a host of the game show *Family Feud.*

R. Lee Ermey (March 24, 1944 —)

Real-life Marine drill instructor R. Lee Ermey won a Golden Globe nomination for his role in *Full Metal Jacket,* and hosted the television series *Mail Call* on weaponry and military history.

Connie Hines (March 24, 1931 — December 18, 2009)

Hines played the wife in the sitcom *Mister Ed.*

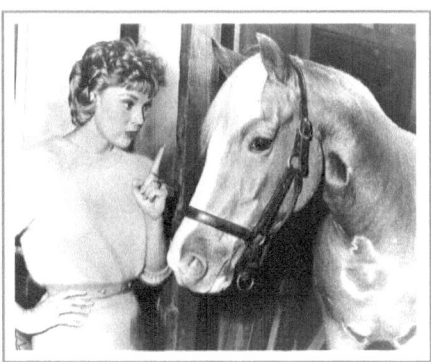

Connie Hines with Mister Ed

Steve McQueen (March 24, 1930 — November 7, 1980)

McQueen was nominated for an Academy Award for The Sand Pebbles, and became the highest-paid movie star in the world for his roles in such films as *The Magnificent Seven, The Great Escape, The Thomas Crown Affair*, and *Bullitt*.

Norman Fell (March 24, 1924 — December 14, 1998)

Fell is best remembered for playing the landlord on the sitcom *Three's Company* and its spinoff *The Ropers*.

Murray Hamilton (March 24, 1923 — September 1, 1986)

Hamilton appeared in such films as *The Hustler, The Graduate, Jaws, The Spirit of St. Loui*s, and *No Time for Sergeants*.

Gene Nelson (March 24, 1920 — September 16, 1996)

Actor, dancer, and director Gene Nelson received two Tony nominations for his Broadway work and played Will Parker in the 1955 film *Oklahoma!* He directed the Elvis Presley films Kissin' Cousins (and co-wrote the screenplay) and Harum Scarum, and directed TV shows including *Star Trek, I Dream of Jeannie*, and *Gunsmoke*.

Richard Conte (**March 24, 1910 — April 15, 1975**)

American actor Conte appeared in such films as *I'll Cry Tomorrow* and *Ocean's 11*, but is best known as Don Barzini in *The Godfather*.

Fatty Arbuckle (**March 24, 1887 — June 29, 1933**)

Fatty Arbuckle (right) in the 1916 film *Bright Lights*

Influential and highly popular silent film star Roscoe "Fatty" Arbuckle was instrumental in discovering and mentoring such talent as Charlie Chaplin, Buster Keaton, and Bob Hope. He was accused of raping and accidentally killing a young actress named Virginia Rappe. After two trials ended in mistrial, he was acquitted in his third trial, receiving a full exoneration and a written apology from the jury. It was too late for his career; his films were banned. He died in 1933 on the verge of a comeback.

Harry Houdini (March 24, 1874 — October 31, 1926)

Legendary magician and escape artist Harry Houdini was famous for his challenge to police officers to try to keep him locked up and for various death defying stunts, including being buried alive.

Harry Houdini publicity poster

Letters

Tabitha Spruce King (March 24, 1949 —)

Tabitha Spruce King has published eight novels and two nonfiction books. She is the wife of author Stephen King.

David Irving (March 24, 1938 —)

World War II historian David Irving authored nearly 30 books on the topic, but his reputation was later discredited because of his Holocaust denial and Nazi sympathies.

Robert Heilbroner (March 24, 1919 — January 4, 2005)

Economist and historian Heilbroner is best known for his 1953 best-seller *The Worldly Philosophers*, covering famous economists from Adam Smith to Karl Marx.

Lawrence Ferlinghetti (March 24, 1919 —)

Poet and bookseller Lawrence Ferlinghetti is best known for his 1958 poetry collection *A Coney Island of the Mind*, which sold over 1 million copies, and as the co-founder of San Francisco's City Lights Booksellers & Publishers. He published Allen Ginsberg's *Howl*, and was arrested on obscenity charges, which were dismissed in a landmark First Amendment case.

Donald Hamilton (March 24, 1916 — November 20, 2006)

Novelist Donald Hamilton is best known for the Matt Helm spy series. The films *The Big Country* and *The Violent Men* were adapted from two of his Westerns.

Malcolm Muggeridge (March 24, 1903 — November 14, 1990)

English journalist, author and media personality Muggeridge snuck reports about the Ukrainian famine out of the Soviet Union, spied during World War II, and helped bring Mother Teresa to fame.

Silas Hocking (March 24 1850 — September 15, 1935)

English children's author Hocking is known for his 1879 best-selling novel *Her Benny*, adapted into a silent film in 1920. He wrote over 50 books.

William Morris (March 24 1834 — October 3, 1896)

Author, illustrator, and textile designer William Morris (left) helped create the modern fantasy genre with his 1896 book *The Well at the World's End*, a direct influence on such authors as J.R.R. Tolkien.

Military and Exploration

John Wesley Powell (March 24 1834 — September 23, 1902)

Soldier and explorer Powell led the 1869 Powell Geographic Expedition, which included the first known passsage through the Grand Canyon, and was later director of the US Geological Survey.

John Wesley Powell

Ignacio Zaragoza (March 24, 1829 — September 8, 1862)

Mexican General Zaragoza is known for defeating the French at the Battle of Puebla on May 5, 1862, the event still celebrated as Cinco de Mayo.

Ignacio Zaragoza

Michiel de Ruyter (March 24, 1607 — April 29, 1676)

Dutch Admiral Michiel de Ruyter fought the English and French during the 17th century Anglo-Dutch Wars, scoring major victories in such engagements as the Raid on the Medway. He was named one of the greatest Dutchmen who ever lived, recognized as a great admiral even by his enemies.

Admiral Michiel de Ruyter

Music and Dance

Sharon Corr (March 24, 1970 —)
Irish singer-songwriter Sharon Corr is a member of
the pop-rock band The Corrs.

Nena (March 24, 1960 —)
German singer and actress Gabriele Kerner, better
known by her stage name, recorded the international
hit single "99 Luftballons."

Billy Stewart (March 24, 1937 — January 17, 1970)
Scat singer Stewart had a series of R&B and pop hits
including "Summertime" and "Secret Love."

Carol Kaye (March 24, 1935 —)
Bass guitarist Kaye was an extremely prolific
recording studio musician whose work can be heard
on such hits as Ritchie Valens' "La Bamba,"
numerous Simon & Garfunkle songs, the Beach Boys'
Pet Sounds album and singles including "Help Me,
Rhonda" and "California Girls," and many others.

Onna White (March 24, 1922 — April 8, 2005)
Onna White was nominated for eight Tony Awards.
She choreographed *The Music Man, 1776,* and *Mame,*
and received an honorary Oscar for choreographing
1968's *Oliver!*

Fanny Crosby (March 24, 1820 — February 12, 1915)

Evangelical mission worker Fanny Crosby was one of the best known figures in American evangelism. Blind from infancy, she became known as the "Queen of Gospel Song Writers," having composed over 8,000 hymns. Among her compositions are "Pass Me Not, O Gentle Savior" and "To God Be the Glory." She was inducted into the Gospel Music Hall of Fame.

Maria Malibran (March 24, 1808 — September 23, 1836)

Mezzo-soprano Malibran (right) was one of the best known opera singers of the 19th century.

Politics and Law

Thomas E. Dewey (March 24, 1902 — January 1, 1958)

New York governor Thomas E. Dewey was the Republican candidate for President of the United States in 1944 and 1948.

In the second race, he lost narrowly to Harry S. Truman, leading to the famous image of Truman holding a copy of the Chicago *Daily Tribune* with the incorrect headline DEWEY BEATS TRUMAN.

Thomas E. Dewey

Horace Gray (March 24, 1828 — September 15, 1902)

Associate Justice of the Supreme Court Horace Gray was the first justice to hire a law clerk.

Matilda Joslyn Gage (March 24, 1826 — March 18, 1898)

Growing up in a house that was a station on the Underground Railroad, Gage became involved in women's right and suffrage. She was president of the National Woman Suffrage Association and founded the Women's National Liberal Union. She co-authored *History of Woman Suffrage* and edited *The National Citizen*. She was the mother-in-law of *Wizard of Oz* creator L. Frank Baum.

Rufus King (March 24, 1755 — April 29, 1827)

King was one of the signers of the United States Constitution, represented New York in the Senate, and ran unsuccessfully for President on the 1816 Federalist ticket.

Thomas Cushing (March 24, 1725 — February 28, 1788)

Cushing was active in Massachusetts protests against British policies and helped Benjamin Franklin work to reduce the rising tensions in the colonies. He was elected to represent his state in the Continental Congress, but was voted out when he opposed independence.

Samuel Ashe (March 24, 1725 — February 3, 1813)

Revolutionary soldier and North Carolina congressman Ashe helped draft the first North Carolina constitution and served as ninth governor of the state. The North Carolina towns of Asheville and Asheboro are named for him.

Science and Technology

David Suzuki (March 24, 1936 —)

Zoologist Suzuki is best known as the host of the Canadian TV science program *The Nature of Things*.

Adolf Butenandt (March 24, 1903 — January 18, 1995)

German chemist Butenandt shared the 1939 Nobel Prize in Chemistry for identifying and isolating the sex hormones estrogen, progesterone, and androsterone. He was a member of the Nazi party and worked on German military projects involving oxygen uptake for high-altitude bomber pilots.

Wilhelm Reich (March 24, 1897 — November 3, 1957)

Austrian psychoanalyst Wilhelm Reich was one of the most controversial and polarizing figures in the history of psychiatry.

Known for his books *The Mass Psychology of Fascism* and *The Sexual Revolution*, his philosophy of sexual permissiveness and postulation of the "orgone" led to his conviction and imprisonment in the US in 1956.

He died in prison; over six tons of his publications were burned by government order, one of the largest examples of censorship in American history.

Marston Morse (March 24, 1892 — June 22, 1977)

American mathematician Marston Morse developed Morse theory, a technique of differential topology that is fundamental to many topics in mathematical physics, including string theory.

Peter Debye (March 24, 1884 — November 2, 1966)

The unit of measurement of molecular dipole moment, the *debye*, is named for Nobel Prize winning chemist Peter Debye. Director of physics at the Kaiser Wilhelm Institute in Berlin, Debye was implicated in a 2006 book as having been active in removing "non-Aryan elements" from German science institutions, a charge that remains controversial. A more recent work claims that Debye may have been a spy for the British MI6; it is known he assisted in the escape of physicist Lise Meitner from Nazi Germany.

Jožef Stefan (March 24, 1835 — January 7, 1893)

Slovene physicist and mathematician Stefan is known for the Stefan-Boltzmann law describing black-body and grey-body radiation.

A.E. Becquerel (March 24, 1820 — May 11, 1891)

French physicist A.E. Becquerel is best known for discovering the photovoltaic effect, fundamental to the operation of a solar cell.

Joseph Liouville (March 24, 1809 — September 8, 1882)

French mathematician Liouville is best known for Liouville's theorem, Liouville numbers, the Sturm-Liouville theory, and the concept of Liouville integrability. He has a crater on the Moon named for him.

John Harrison (March 24, 1693 — March 24, 1776)

English clockmaker John Harrison invented the first practical marine chronometer, a clock with enough accuracy to be used in establishing the longitude of a ship. The British Parliament had offered a prize of £20,000 (almost £3 million today) for the solution. He was born and died on March 24.

Georgius Agricola (March 24, 1494 — November 21, 1555)

German scientist Georgius Agricola is known as the "father of minerology," and his treatise on mining and metallurgy, *De re metallica*, was the standard reference work on the topic for over two centuries.

Sports and Chess

Starlin Castro (March 24, 1990 —)

Cubs shortstop Castro hold the RBI record for a Major League debut and is the youngest player to lead the National League in hits.

Chris Bosh (March 24, 1984 —)

Nicknamed "CB4," Bosh played for the Toronto Raptors and the Miami Heat, and was part of the 2008 Olympic gold medal basketball team.

Dustin McGowan (March 24, 1982 —)

Pitcher McGowan plays for the Toronto Blue Jays.

Corey Hart (March 24, 1982 —)

Outfielder Corey Hart plays for the Milwaukee Brewers.

Dirk Hayhurst (March 24, 1981 —)

Former MLB pitcher Hayhurst hit the New York *Times* Bestseller List with his book *The Bullpen Gospels* about his time in the minor leagues.

Peyton Manning (March 24, 1976 —)

Quarterback Peyton Manning played for the Denver Broncos and the Indianapolis Colts, winning a record four league MVP awards.

Aaron Brooks (March 24, 1976 —)

Quarterback Aaron Brooks played for the Green Bay Packers, the New Orleans Saints, and the Oakland Raiders.

Thomas Johansson (March 24, 1974 —)

Swedish tennis grand slam champion Johansson won the Australian Open in 2002 and received a silver medal at the 2008 Olympic Games.

Steve Karsay (March 24, 1972 —)

Pitcher Karsay played for the Oakland Athletics, the Cleveland Indians, the Atlanta Braves, and the New York Yankees.

The Undertaker (March 24, 1965 —)

Wrestler Mark Calaway is best known by his ring name The Undertaker.

Scott Pruett (March 24, 1960 —)

Pruett won ten go kart championships and was inducted into the World Karting Hall of Fame. He raced professionally in NASCAR, Champ Car, IMSA, Trans-Am, and Grand-Am, wrote children's books, and founded the winery Pruett Vineyards.

Mike Woodson (March 24, 1968 —)

Former basketball player Mike Woodson became head coach of the New York Knicks in 2011.

Pat Bradley (March 24, 1951 —)

Pat Bradley won six major golf championships and was elected to the World Golf Hall of Fame in 1991.

Dennis Erickson (March 24, 1947 —)

Football coach Dennis Erickson was head coach of Arizona State University, the University of Idaho, the Seattle Seahawks, and the San Francisco 49ers.

Vasily Smyslov (Василий Смыслов) (March 24, 1921 — March 27, 2010)

Smyslov was World Chess Champion from 1957 to 1958, and won an all-time record of 17 Chess Olympiad medals. A character in *2001: A Space Odyssey* is named for him.

George Wagner (March 24, 1915 — December 26, 1963)

Professional wrestler "Gorgeous George" Wagner gained wide popularity for his flamboyant media personality. He was inducted into both the Professional Wrestling Hall of Fame and the WWE Hall of Fame.

George Sisler (March 24, 1893 — March 26, 1973)

"Gentleman George" (also known as "Gorgeous George") Sisler (left) was a first baseman for the St. Louis Browns and the Washington Senators, and elected to the Baseball Hall of Fame in 1939. He played for the University of Michigan in college. He is listed by *The Sporting News* as one of baseball's 100 greatest players of all time.

Albert Hill (March 24, 1889 — January 8, 1969)

British long distance runner Albert Hill won two gold medals in the 1920 Summer Olympics.

Who Died on March 24?

Arts

Ivan Kramskoi (Ивáн Крамскóй) (June 8 [O.S. May 27], 1837 — March 24 [O.S. April 6], 1887)

Painter and art critic Ivan Kramskoi is known for his portraits of important Russian writers, scientists, and other public figures, and was a leading figure of the Russian democratic art movement.

Self-portrait by Ivan Kramskoi

Chess

Alexander Alekhine (Алекса́ндр Але́хин) (October 31 [O.S. October 19], 1837 — March 24, 1946)

Widely considered one of the greatest chess players in history, reigning as world champion for a total of 17 years after defeating José Capablanca. As a chess author and theoretician, he created innovative chess openings, and developed the strategy known as Alekhine's Defence.

Film, Television, and Radio

Robert Culp (August 16, 1930 — March 24, 2010)

Culp is best known for his role on the espionage series *I Spy*, and for movie roles in *PT 109*, *Bob & Carol & Ted & Alice*, and *The Pelican Brief*.

Richard Widmark (December 26, 1914 — March 24, 2008)

Widmark was nominated for an Oscar for his debut role in *Kiss of Death*, and appeared in over 60 films including *Yellow Sky*, *No Way Out*, *The Bedford Incident*, *The Alamo*, *Judgment at Nuremberg*, and *How the West Was Won*.

Richard Widmark in *Panic in the Streets*

Hal Riney (July 17, 1932 — March 24, 2008)

Advertising Hall of Fame member Hal Riney hired Paul Williams to write a song for a bank commercial that became The Carpenters hit "We've Only Just Begun," created the "Morning in America" and "Bear in the Woods" commercials for the Ronald Reagan 1984 Presidential Campaign, and developed the Bartles & Jaymes campaign for E & J Gallo Winery.

Lynne Perrie (April 7, 1931 — March 24, 2006)

Perrie was known to English audiences as Ivy Tilsley in the long-running soap opera *Coronation Street*.

Ray Goulding (March 20, 1922 — March 24, 1990)

Goulding and Bob Elliott formed the radio comedy duo of Bob and Ray.

Sam Jaffe (March 10, 1891 — March 24, 1984)

Actor Sam Jaffe was nominated for an Oscar for his role in the 1950 film *The Asphalt Jungle*. He appeared in such films as *Ben-Hur, The Day the Earth Stood Still, Gunga Din* (in the title role), and *Lost Horizon*. He also co-starred in the long-running television series *Ben Casey*.

Alice Guy-Blaché (July 1, 1873 — March 24, 1968)

French director Guy-Blaché was the first female director in the motion picture industry, as well as one of the first directors of a fiction film. In a 24 year career, she directed over 400 films (22 feature length) and became the first (and so far only) woman to own and manage her own studio.

Heroism

Pierlucio Tinazzi (December 27, 1962 — March 24, 1999)

Tinazzi was a hero of the Mont Blanc tunnel fire of 1999, which killed 37 people out of 50 who were trapped in the blaze. Of the 12 survivors, Tinazzi, an Italian security guard, rescued ten by riding into the tunnel on his motorcycle and bringing out people one by one. He died trying to save an unconscious man who was too big to carry, and his motorcycle melted into the pavement beside him.

Letters

Martin Caidin (September 14, 1927 — March 24, 1997)

Caidin wrote over 50 books on aeronautics and aviation, winning numerous awards; and also wrote such science novels as *Marooned* and *Cyborg*.

John Hersey (June 17, 1914 — March 24, 1993)

Journalist John Hersey came to prominence for his 1946 article "Hiroshima," about the atomic bombing of the Japanese city (later published as a book), which took up an entire issue of *The New Yorker*, the only article to ever do so.

He won the Pulitzer Prize for his first novel, *A Bell for Adano*. An article he wrote about the dullness of grammar school readers inspired Dr. Seuss to write *The Cat in the Hat*.

John Millington Synge (April 16, 1871 — March 24, 1909)

Irish playwright and poet Synge is best known for *The Playboy of the Western World*, a then-controversial play that caused riots during its first production in Dublin in 1907.

Jules Verne (February 8, 1828 — March 24, 1905)

French author Jules Verne was an early figure in the development of modern science fiction, and is (after Agatha Christie) the most translated author in the world. His works include *Twenty Thousand Leagues Under the Sea* and *Around the World in Eighty Days*.

Jules Verne, photograph by Félix Nadar

Henry Wadsworth Longfellow
(February 27, 1807 — March 24, 1882)

American poet Henry Wadsworth Longfellow is known for such works as *Paul Revere's Ride, The Song of Hiawatha,* and *Evangeline.*

Henry Wadsworth Longfellow

Military

Bernard Law Montgomery, 1ˢᵗ Viscount Montgomery of Alamein (November 17, 1887 — March 24, 1976)

British Field Marshal Bernard Montgomery oversaw planning of D-Day and commanded all Allied ground forces from the initial landing to the end of the Battle of Normandy. He commanded the 21st Army Group in northwest Europe and accepted the German surrender.

Bernard Montgomery

Orde Wingate (**February 26, 1903 —**
March 24, 1944)

British Major-General Orde Wingate is considered
one of the founders of modern guerrilla warfare.
During World War II, he created the Chindits, a
British India special operations force that operated
deep behind enemy lines. A religious Christian, he
was also a strong Zionist, and trained members of
the Haganah paramilitary organization that became
part of the Jewish Resistance Movement that led to
the founding of the state of Israel.

Antoine-Henri Jomini (**March 6, 1779**
— March 24, 1869)

Baron Jomini was a general in the French and later
the Russian armies during the Napoleonic Wars, and
wrote a notable book on military strategy and tactics,
Précis de l'Art de la Guerre, or *The Art of War*, which
influenced generals on both sides during the
American Civil War.

Music

Johnny Maestro (**May 7, 1939 — March**
24, 2010)

Johnny Maestro founded and led the group Johnny
Maestro and The Brooklyn Bridge, who had a
million-selling hit with 1968's "The Worst That
Could Happen."

Neil Aspinall (October 13, 1941 — March 24, 2008)

British music executive Aspinall went to school with Paul McCartney and George Harrison, and later headed the Beatles's company Apple Corps.

Chalmers "Spanky" Alford (May 22, 1955 — March 24, 2008)

Jazz guitarist Spanky Alford won three Grammys in his career. He was part of the gospel group Mighty Clouds of Joy, the neo-soul group The Soultronics, and played on albums by the Bee Gees, Al Green, Mary J. Blige, and A Tribe Called Quest.

Harold Melvin (June 25, 1939 — March 24, 1997)

Harold Melvin founded and led the doo-wop/R&B group Harold Melvin & the Blue Notes, whose hits included "If You Don't Know Me By Now," "The Love I Lost," and "Wake Up Everybody."

Jean Goldkette (March 18, 1893 — March 24, 1962)

Critics say that influential early jazz bandleader Jean Goldkette's innovative arrangements made his band "the first original white swing band in jazz history." Musicians including Bix Beiderbecke, Hoagy Carmichael, Tommy Dorsey, and many others played in Goldkette's bands.

Politics

Mary of Teck, Queen Consort of England (May 26, 1867 — March 24, 1953)

Mary of Teck was married to King-Emperor George V of England. Her eldest son Edward VIII abdicated the throne to marry American socialite Wallis Simpson. Her second son became King George VI, and her granddaughter became Queen Elizabeth II.

Elizabeth I of England (September 7, 1533 — March 24, 1603)

Elizabeth I was the daughter of Henry VIII and Anne Boleyn, and was initially passed over for the throne, and became Queen of England and Ireland at the age of 25, ruling for 44 years.

Her reign as the "Virgin Queen" or "Good Queen Bess" is now known as the Elizabethan era, marked by the plays of William Shakespeare, the adventures and explorations of Sir Francis Drake, and the defeat of the Spanish Armada.

Because she never married or had children, on her death the throne went to James I of Scotland (James VI of England and Ireland), son of her cousin and enemy Mary Queen of Scots.

The "Sieve Portrait" of Queen Elizabeth I
by Quentin Metsys the Younger

Harun al-Rashid (هارون الرشي) (c. March 17, 763 — March 24, 809)

Caliph Harun al-Rashid (Aaron the Just) of the Abbasid dynasty ruled what became modern Iraq during a period of prosperity and cultural growth, building Baghdad into one of the most important cities in the world. He founded the intellectual center known as Bayt al-Hikma (بيت الحكمة), or the House of Wisdom, where modern algebra, the first programmable machine, and major medical advances originated. The House of Wisdom lasted for centuries, until it was destroyed during the Mongol invasion of Baghdad in 1258. Harun al-Rashid became a figure of legend for his role in the Arabian Nights (*The Book of a Thousand Nights and a Night*).

Religion

Óscar Romero (August 15, 1917 — March 24, 1980)

Catholic Archishop Óscar Romero of El Salvador was assassinated for protesting human rights abuses of the government and military. His funeral, attended by over 250,000, was attacked with smoke bombs and rifle fire. While no one was prosecuted for either event, many believe government death squads were responsible. He has been proposed as a candidate for sainthood.

Joseph ben Ephraim Karo (1488 — March 24, 1575)

Rabbi Yosef Karo compiled the *Shulchan Aruch*, a codification of Jewish law that remains authoritative in the Jewish world. He is often referred to as HaMachaber ("The Author") or Maran ("Our Master") for his achievements.

Science

César Milstein (October 8, 1927 — March 24, 2002)

Argentine biochemist Milstein shared the 1984 Nobel Prize in Physiology or Medicine for his discovery of the principle of production of monoclonal antibodies.

Auguste Piccard (January 28, 1884 — March 24, 1962)

The Piccard brothers, Auguste and Jean Felix, were scientists and explorers. Auguste Piccarde was a physics professor who did pioneering work in the measurement of cosmic rays.

In addition, he made a series of record-setting balloon flights in a pressurized gondola of his own design, achieving an altitude of 23,000 meters (over 75,000 feet); and invented the bathyscape, allowing deep sea exploration.

The *Star Trek* captain Jean-Luc Picard is named for the Piccard brothers, and the character Professor Cuthbert Calculus in *The Adventure of Tintin* is based on Auguste Piccard.

Sports

Jocky Wilson (March 22, 1950 — March 24, 2012)

Wilson won the World Professional Darts Championship in 1982 and 1989.

George Kell (August 23, 1922 — March 24, 2009)

Baseball Hall of Fame member George Kell played for the Philadelphia Athletics, Detroit Tigers, Boston Red Sox, Chicago White Sox, and the Baltimore Orioles before becoming a baseball broadcaster for 40 years.

Birdie Tebbetts (November 10, 1912 — March 24, 1999)

After a successful career in which he was considered the best catcher in the American League, Tebbetts became the manager of the Cincinnati Reds, the Milwaukee Braves, and the Cleveland Indians. He was the National League Manager of the Year in 1956.

Bowman baseball card of Birdie Tebbetts, 1952

Carl Schuhmann (May 12, 1869 — March 24, 1946)

German gymnast, wrestler, and weightlifter Schuhmann won four gold medals at the first modern Olympic Games in Athens in 1896, becoming the most successful athlete in those games.

March: The Third Month

"Up from the sea, the wild north wind is blowing
Under the sky's gray arch;
Smiling I watch the shaken elm boughs, knowing
It is the wind of March."

— "March," John Greenleaf Whittier

In ancient Rome, March was the first month of the year. As the first month of spring, in the Mediterranean climate it marked the beginning of the military campaign season. That's why March (Martius) is named in honor of Mars, the Roman god of war.

Although the first month of the year was moved back to January sometime during the transition of Rome from a kingdom to a republic (historians differ), March was the first month of the year in Russia until the end of the 15th Century, and is the first month of the year in many other cultures and religions.

In the northern hemisphere, March 1 marks the beginning of meteorological spring. In the southern hemisphere, March is the equivalent of September, making southern hemisphere March the beginning of autumn.

March is one of the seven months that have 31 days in it. March starts on the same day of the week as November every year, and except for leap years starts on the same day as February. March starts on the same day of the week as the previous June except for leap years, and in leap years starts on the same day as the previous September and December.

March in Other Cultures

In Finland, March is called *maaliskuu* (earthy month). In Ukraine, it's *березень* (birch tree). Other names for March include *Lentmonat* (Saxon), *Hyld-monath* (Angles), and *sušec* (Slovene).

March Symbols

Birthstones: Aquamarine (right) and bloodstone, both representing courage.

Birth Flowers: Daffodils

March Events

Honorary months

Presidents, Congresses, and nations around the world issue proclamations recognizing particular months to honor certain causes. These events generally fall in March. (All US unless otherwise noted.)

National Nutrition Month

American Red Cross Month

Women's History Month (celebrated in Canada during October)

Irish-American Heritage Month

Colorectal Cancer Awareness Month

Fire Prevention Month (The Philippines)

"March Madness" (United States)

The NCAA Men's Division I Basketball Championship, popularly known as "March Madness" or the "Big Dance," is a single-elimination tournament to establish the champion college basketball team.

Earth Hour (International)

On Earth Hour, held on the last Saturday of March each year, households and business are urged to turn off all non-essential lights for one hour between 8:30pm to 9:30pm on each person's local time. The goal is to raise awareness of the need to take action on climate change.

Easter Events

La crucifixión by El Greco

Easter Season

The Christian holiday of Easter in Western Christianity is held on the first Sunday after the Paschal Full Moon following the March equinox, which is officially set at March 21 by church reckoning. Easter itself can therefore occur as early as March 22 and as late as April 25, but occurs most often in April.

In Eastern Christianity, which uses the Julian calendar, Easter occurs between April 4 and May 8. This also sets the date for the various events that lead up to Easter, most importantly the events of Holy Week.

Passion Sunday

The fifth Sunday of the Christian season of Lent is known as Passion Sunday in various Protestant denominations and by some traditionalist Catholics. Sometimes, the sixth Sunday of Lent is referred to as Passion Sunday, but it is more commonly known as Palm Sunday.

Passion Sunday starts the two-week Passiontide, which ends on Holy Saturday, the day before Easter, commemorating the day that Jesus's body was laid in the tomb. The fifth Sunday of Lent can occur as early as March 8 (though the next time it will be that early is in 2285 CE), and as late as April 11.

Palm Sunday

The moveable feast of Palm Sunday commemorates the triumphant entry of Jesus into Jerusalem, an event mentioned in all four gospels. In many Christian churches, palm leaves are distributed to the worshippers. The earliest date for Palm Sunday is March 15, and the latest is April 18.

Maundy Thursday

The Thursday before Easter is Maundy Thursday, when the Last Supper took place. Because of its relation to Easter, the earliest day it can occur is March 19, and the latest it can occur is April 22.

Good Friday

Good Friday, observed during Holy Week on the Friday preceding Easter Sunday, commemorates the crucifixion of Jesus and his death at Calvary. Because of its relation to Easter, the earliest day it can occur is March 20, and the latest it can occur is April 23.

Holy Saturday

Sometimes called Easter Eve or Black Saturday, Holy Saturday commemorates the day in which Jesus's body lay in the tomb.

Some mistakenly refer to this day as "Easter Saturday," but that properly describes the Saturday following Easter, the last day of Easter Week. The earliest it can occur is March 21, and the latest it can occur is April 24.

Easter

Easter celebrates the resurrection of Jesus Christ on the third day after his crucifixion. In the liturgical calendar, Easter follows the season of Lent, and begins the period known as Eastertide, which ends on Pentecost Sunday.

Easter is observed religiously in a morning service. In the U.S., it's also common to decorate Easter eggs (right) and make Easter baskets of eggs and candy, often  with the Easter bunny as a symbol. The White House traditionally hosts an egg hunt, and many communities have Easter parades.

Easter customs around the world include bonfires (Cyprus, western Sweden), egg fighting (Bulgaria), cross-country skiing and reading murder mysteries (Norway), and children dressed as witches collecting candy door-to-door (other Nordic countries).

Easter Monday

In some Roman Catholic and Eastern Orthodox cultures, the Monday after Easter is celebrated as a holiday. It is also known as **Egg Nyte**, featuring egg rolling competitions and dousing other people with water that had been blessed with holy water the previous day at mass. Easter Monday is also celebrated as **Family Day** in South Africa. In Guyana, people fly kites that were made on Holy Saturday. In Portugal, it is known as the **Anjo (Ivy) Festival**, in which people picnic in the countryside.

Smigus-Dyngus (Poland, Hungary, Czech Republic, Slovakia)

The Monday after Easter in Poland and in the Polish diaspora is known as **Śmigus-Dyngus,** or simply Dyngus Day in the U.S.. Boys throw water over girls they like and spank them with pussy willows. Girls avoid getting wet by giving boys "ransoms" of painted eggs.

Easter Week

The period from Easter Sunday to the following Saturday is known as **Easter Week**. In both Western and Eastern Christianity (where it's known as **Bright Week**), the resurrection continues to be celebrated in church services. **Easter Tuesday** is a public holiday in the Australian state of Tasmania.

March Zodiac Signs

From the perspective of someone on Earth, the Sun appears to move through the sky throughout the year, along a path astronomers call the ecliptic plane. The ecliptic plane is divided into twelve constellations, known as the zodiac, based on traditionally observed patterns of stars. On your birthday, you can't see your constellation, because it's part of the daytime sky.

The zodiac was first developed by Babylonian astronomers about 2,500 years ago. Because they were unaware that the Earth wobbles like a spinning top (a motion known as *precession*), they didn't make allowance for the fact that the Sun's path through the zodiac changes over time.

That means there are now two sets of dates for your birth sign. The *tropical* dates are the original Babylonian dates; the *siderial* dates tell you where the Sun actually appears as it moves along its annual path.

In siderial reckoning, March 24 is in Pisces, but in tropical astrology, March 24 in in Aries.

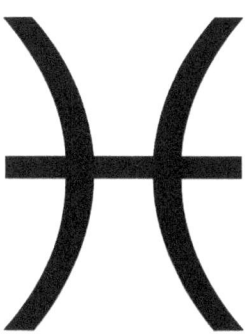

Pisces

Tropical February 20 to March 20

Siderial March 15 to April 14

In the Roman legend of Venus and her son Cupid, they escaped the clutches of Typhon, known as the "father of all monsters," by transforming into fish and tying themselves together with rope. That's why the name Pisces is plural for fish. The constellation appears as a somewhat ragged "V" shape, representing the rope, with the "fish" located at the two rope ends.

In astrology, Pisces is a water sign, compatible with the other water signs Cancer and Scorpio, as well as with the earth signs Taurus, Virgo, and Capricorn. Pisceans are supposed to be imaginative, compassionate, unworldly, secretive, and escapist.

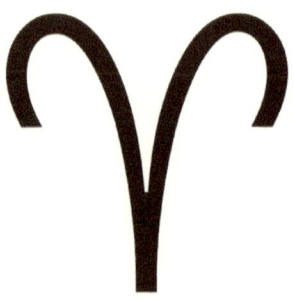

Aries

Tropical March 21 to April 19

Siderial April 15 to May 15

In Greek mythology, Aries is a ram with golden wings and golden wool who rescued the twins Phrixus and Helle from certain death. Although Helle died in the rescue attempt, the grateful Phrixus sacrificed the ram to Zeus. The golden fleece from the sacrificed ram played a prominent part in the later myth of Jason and the Argonauts.

In astrology, Aries, a fire sign, is compatible with the other fire signs of Gemini, Leo, and Sagittarius, and to a lesser extent with air signs Scorpio and Libra. Arians are supposed to adventurous, enthusiastic, quick-tempered, and impulsive.

What Day of the Week is March 24?

On what day of the week does March 24 fall?

Surprisingly, this isn't an easy question. Because the calendar year is 365 days long (366 in leap years), it doesn't divide evenly by the seven days of the week.

Also, the Earth goes around the Sun in about 365-1/4 days, so a calendar tends to drift over time. That's why the same date falls on different weekdays in different years.

This is made even more complicated by a change in calendars that took place in 1582. Our modern calendar has its roots in ancient Rome, in a calendar reform conducted by Julius Caesar. Caesar commissioned mathematicians to attack the problem, and came up with the idea of *leap years*, and thus standardized the calendar for centuries to come. This was called the *Julian calendar.*

Over time, however, the small errors in Caesar's calculation compounded. That's why Pope Gregory XIII commissioned the *Gregorian calendar,* used in most of the world today. Some countries converted in 1582, when the calendar was first developed; some converted later; other still haven't changed.

Gregorian and Julian aren't the only types of calendars. The Hebrew year, the Islamic year, and many other calendars are used in different parts of the world and among different people.

You can convert Gregorian dates to other calendars, including the Hebrew calendar, the Islamic calendar, and even the Mayan calendar by visiting the Fourmilab Calendar Converter at http://www.fourmilab.ch/documents/calendar/.

A 50-year brass perpetual calendar.

Copyright, Credit, and Contact

Follow Us

Our blog Dobson's Improbable History features short articles on events and people associated with each day, and updates several times each week. Get the latest on Twitter @SidewiseThinker.

Contact Us

Find an error or a format problem? Want information about the series, about us, or about when the volume for your special day might be available? Please email us at editor@timespinnerpress.com.

Sources and Art Credits

We are grateful to Wikipedia, which is our first stop for research. We attempt to make independent confirmation of all important dates and facts through a variety of other sources.

All art and photographs are either in the public domain or used under a Creative Commons license, and most frequently come from Wikimedia Commons. Attribution is provided where requested by the copyright owner or when of historical significance, listed below.

- The cover illustration of Tokugawa Ieyasu was created in the 18th century by 投稿者本人が作成, and is in the public domain because its copyright has expired both in Japan and in the US.

- The photograph of a reënactor playing Tokugawa at the Ieyasu Parade was taken by Sacha Zemp, who has released the rights to use the work for any purpose.

- The painting of King James VI and I by Daniel Mytens is in the public domain because its copyright has expired.

- The publicity photograph of Elvis Presley in *Jailhouse Rock* is in the public domain because it was published in the US between 1923 and 1963 and its copyright, if one originally existed, was not renewed.

- The artist's rendition of Ranger 9 about to impact on the Moon is in the public domain as a work of NASA. The name of the artist is unknown.

- The painting of Comet Shoemaker-Levy 9 colliding with Jupiter is by Don Davis, and is used here because it was released into the public domain by the artist.

- The 1923 photograph of Edward Weston and Marguerite Mather by Imogen Cunningham is in the public domain because its copyright has expired. The original is in the Yale University Art Gallery.

- The 1828 self-portrait of Orest Kiprensky is in the public domain because its copyright has expired. The original is in the Tretyakov Gallery, Moscow.

- The 2010 photograph of Steve Ballmer was taken by Microsoft Sweden, and is used here under the Creative Commons Attribution 2.0 Generic license.

- The photograph of George Francis Train was taken by Mathew Brady and is in the collection of the Library of Congress Prints and Photographs Division. It is in the public domain because its copyright has expired.

- The photograph of Bonnie and Clyde was taken sometime between 1932 and 1934. It is in the collection of the Library of Congress Prints and Photographs Division. It is in the public domain because it was published in the US between 1923 and 1977 without a copyright notice.

- The 2004 photograph of Amber Benson and Alyson Hannigan was taken by Raven Underwood and is used here under the Creative Commons Attribution 2.0 Generic license.

- The publicity photograph of Connie Hines with Mister Ed is in the public domain because it was published in the US between 1923 and 1977 without a copyright notice.

- The advertisement for the 1916 film *Bright Lights* is in the public domain because its copyright has expired. It is in the collection of the Library of Congress Prints and Photographs Division.

- The advertisement for a Harry Houdini performance is

in the public domain because its copyright has expired. It is in the collection of the Library of Congress Prints and Photographs Division.

- The 1889 portrait photograph of William Morris was taken by Frederick Hollyer. It is in the public domain because its copyright has expired.

- The photograph of John Wesley Powell is in the public domain as a work of the US government.

- The photograph of Ignacio Zaragoza is from the Colleción Museo de Historia Mexicana, and was released into the public domain by the copyright holder.

- The 1668 painting of Michiel de Ruyter by Hendrick Berckman is in the public domain because its copyright has expired.

- The portrait of Maria Malabran as Desdemona by Henri Decaisne is in the public domain because its copyright has expired. The original is in the Carnavalet Museum in Paris.

- The 1948 photograph of Thomas E. Dewey is part of the New York *World-Telegram & Sun* collection at the Library of Congress Prints and Photographs Division. Per deed of gift, all rights in this photograph were deeded to the public upon its donation to the Library.

- The 1914 photograph of George Sisler is in the public domain because its copyright has expired.

- The 1867 self-portrait of Ivan Kramskoi is in the public domain because its copyright has expired. The original is in the Tretyakov Gallery.

- The screenshot from the trailer for the 1950 film *Panic in the Streets* is in the public domain because it was published in the US between 1923 and 1963, and the copyright (if one originally existed) was not renewed.

- The photograph of Jules Verne by Félix Nadar is in the public domain because its copyright has expired.

- The 1868 photograph of Henry Wadsworth Longfellow by Julia Cameron is in the public domain because its copyright has expired.

- The photograph of Bernard Montgomery in North Africa is in the public domain as work of the US federal government.

- The 1583 "Sieve Portrait" of Queen Elizabeth I is by Quentin Metsys the Younger, and is in the Pinacoteca Nazionale di Siena. It is in the public domain because its copyright has expired.

- The 1952 Bowman baseball card of Birdie Tibbetts is in the public domain because it was published in the US between 1923 and 1963, and the copyright was not renewed.

- The illustration of the month of March used on the back cover and in the interior is from the French Gothic illuminated manuscript *Les Très Riches Heures du duc de Berry* by the Limbourg Brothers, Jean Colombe, and an intermediate painter whose name is lost to history. It is in the public domain because its copyright has expired.

- The photograph of aquamarine has been released into the public domain.

- The photograph of a daffodil is by Javier Martin and is

- The 1917 Women's Suffrage demonstration comes from the Library of Congress, Prints and Photographs Division, LC-USZ62-31799 DLC, and is in the public domain because its copyright has expired.

- The painting *La crucifixión* by El Greco is located in the Museo del Prado. It is in the public domain because its copyright has expired.

- The photograph of Czechoslovakian Easter eggs was taken by Jan Kameníček, who has released the image into the public domain.

- The 50-year perpetual calendar photograph is in the public domain.

Timespinner
Press